The
Best
Trivia Book
ever
written!!!

"Queen of Trivia's"

The
Best
Trivia Book
ever
written!!!

TRIVIA TRIVIA TRIVIA

by the Queen of Trivia

Jane C. Flinn

THE BEST TRIVIA BOOK EVER WRITTEN!!!

a book of trivia and fun facts...

by the
"Queen of Trivia"

Jane C. Flinn

WHAT'S INSIDE

Over the past twenty years, I have sifted through trivia on a wide array of subjects, and have included in this book only what I consider the most exciting trivia ever compiled into one trivia book. Hence, the name, "The Best Trivia Book Ever Written!!!"

TRIVIA & FUN FACTS — MORE POPULAR THAN EVER...

Trivia has never been more popular as a means of self-education, learning and sheer fun — and let's not forget — just a great conversation starter!!!

"Queen of Trivia" is known as the "Mother Goose of Modern-Day Trivia."

Look for more of "Queen of Trivia's" exciting trivia books, including:

The Best Trivia Book Ever!!!

The Best Trivia Book Geography!!!

The Best Trivia Book History!!!

The Best Trivia Book United States Presidents!!!

The Best Trivia Book Fun Facts!!!

The Best Trivia Book Ever Written!!!

For the trivia buff in all of us . . .

Enjoy this trivia book!!!
"Queen of Trivia"

WELCOME!!!

POTPOURRI

1. Where is the one place where a flag flies all day, never goes up or down and does not get saluted?

2. In 1961 the USSR beat the USA into space by how many days?

3. What is the only species of deer where both male and female have antlers?

4. What is London's Big Ben?

5. The first one of these was black and made of charcoal mixed with oil?
(This products' manufacturer was Binney and Smith. It was produced in 1903.)

6. The Panama Canal has 12 locks. The Suez Canal at 101 miles long is twice as long. How many locks does the Suez Canal have?

7. How much did the first ballpoint pens sell for?

1. On the moon

2. 23 days

3. Caribou

4. Bell in the clock tower

5. The first Crayola crayon

6. There are no locks. This is because the Mediterranean Sea and the Gulf of Suez have about the same water level.

7. When they came out in the year 1945, they sold for $12.00. 5,000 people jammed the entrance of New York's Gimbels for the first ballpoint pens.

DID YOU KNOW:
The bikini came out a year later in 1946.

1. Washington has the most unusual State gem; what is this?

2. In what country did the windmill originate?

3. Before Beethoven sat down to compose, what did he do?

4. Who did Olive Oyl date before Popeye?

5. What is an alligator pear?

6. Cheetah and gorilla both make this sound; what is this?

7. Where do fish get their oxygen?

8. What is the only mammal that can live on Eucalyptus?

9. What gland has a lot to do with your growth?

1. Petrified Wood is the official gemstone of Washington.

2. Iran. Originally it was used to grind grain. The windmill originated in 644 AD.

3. He would pour buckets of cold water over his head to fight off fatigue.

4. Ham Gravy. He was her boyfriend in the late 1920s, early '30s.

5. Avocado

6. They purr.

7. From the water, because fish are equipped with gills and not lungs.

8. Koala

9. Pituitary

1. 100,000 chemical reactions occur in the brain every second, every minute or every hour?

2. What cheese is the Water Buffalo's milk used to make?

3. Where in your body do you have the most sweat glands?

4. For the first 35 years of Mr. Potato Head's life, he had this accessory. Then in 1987, this was taken away. What was this?

5. What is the only thing that Phil Mickelson does that is left-handed?

6. This game was originally played with a soccer ball and two bushel baskets.

7. For the above, what is the only thing that has changed?

8. Which is drier, the moon or the Gobi Desert?

1. Every second the brain stem (medulla oblongata) controls many of your automatic actions such as your heart beat and breathing.

2. This is the traditional way of making Mozzarella Cheese.

3. Your feet; there's 250,000 sweat glands in your feet.

4. His pipe

5. Swing a club

6. Basketball

7. Originally, there were nine players on each team, now there are only five.

8. The moon is one million times drier.

1. Name the flower that has more varieties than any other.

2. What part of the potato plant do we eat?

3. What is the nut that is technically a kernel from a pear-shaped "false" fruit?

4. Michelangelo was 26 when he began sculpting this statue.

5. What is the approximate speed that most commercial jets take off and land?

6. What song written by Paul Anka was recorded by Frank Sinatra and Elvis Presley?

7. The Liberty Bell weighs over one ton. How many pounds is a ton?

DID YOU KNOW:
The world's largest mammal, the blue whale, weighs close to 3 tons at birth.

1. *Orchid; there are at least 30,000.*

2. *The part that grows underground, the potato tuber. The fruits and leaves of the potato plant which grow above the ground are poisonous.*

3. *The cashew nut*

4. *David. In 1501 he started this, and he completed this in 1504.*

5. *160 mph*

6. *My Way*

7. *2,000 pounds*

SCIENCE

1. On what planet is the largest known volcano?

2. What is found in matches that is also found in the human body?

3. What is the everyday term for calcium carbonate?

4. What is the common name for hydrogen oxide?

   DID YOU KNOW:
   There are 169 known moons in our solar system.

5. What was once used as transmission oil in the Rolls Royce?

6. What is unique about snow flakes and spider webs?

7. In 1828 what metal was used to make coins in Russia?

8. How old was Einstein when he developed the Theory of Relativity?

1. Mars. The largest known volcano in our solar system is on Mars; this is Olympus Mons. At 88,600 feet high, and 335 miles across, it is three times as tall as Mount Everest.

In comparison, the largest volcano on earth is Hawaii's Mauna Loa at 74 miles across and about 32,000 feet high, rising from the ocean.

2. Phosphorous. This is found in every cell of the human body. Like calcium, it helps in the formation of strong bones and teeth.

3. Chalk

4. Water

5. Spermaceti Oil from the Sperm Whale

6. No two are alike. You can also include elephant ears in this category.

7. Platinum; it wasn't highly valued at the time.

8. 26

1. What was the code name of the atomic bomb that was dropped on Hiroshima on August 6, 1945?

2. How fast does lightning travel?

3. What was named the Great Tabular?

4. On which celestial body would you weigh more?

a) Moon   b) Sun

5. Is it true that most of the gas we breathe is oxygen?

6. The giant planets are Jupiter, Saturn, _ _ _ _ _ _ and Neptune.

7. How are a sundial and an hourglass so different?

1. *Little Boy*

2. *Lightning bolts travel up to 75 miles a second.*

3. *Iceberg. This vast flat shelf of ice was about the same size as Rhode Island. After breaking off from its glacier, an iceberg will last between one and three years.*

DID YOU KNOW: Geologists can ascertain which glacier an iceberg came from by studying its crystal structure.

4. *b) On the Sun. If you weigh 2,800 pounds on the Sun, you would weigh 17 pounds on the Moon.*

5. *This is false. 78% of the air we breathe is nitrogen gas. Less than one percent is argon and other gases. The only gas in the air which is used by our bodies is oxygen.*

6. *Uranus. No spacecraft could ever land on these super giants; the reason is because they are made mostly of liquid gas, unlike the other planets which are comprised of rock.*

7. *A sundial is a timepiece with the least moving parts, and an hourglass has the most moving parts, as it is filled with many grains of sand.*

1. What is significant about minus 459 degrees Fahrenheit?

2. _ _ _ o_ _ n _ has no specific freezing point. It freezes at any temperature between 180 degrees and 240 degrees Farenheit. Even when it does freeze, it never solidifies totally, but resembles gum or wax.

3. Earth orbits the sun once every

a) day   b) month   c) year

4. If the sun is a star that's like the others, why does it look so different?

   DID YOU KNOW: 1.3 million Earths could fit inside our sun. The sun is 863,000 miles wide.

5. Which planet has three of the five largest moons?

_ _ _ _ _ _ _ _

6. Name the only substance that when freezing will expand, instead of contract.

7. What is the layer of atmosphere that we live in?

1. *This is the coldest temperature that anything can ever reach.*

2. *Gasoline*

3. *c) year*

4. *It is so close to Earth; it is only 93 million miles away! That is close when you consider that the next closest star to us is 25 trillion miles away.*

5. *Jupiter has 63 moons; Ganymede, Callisto and Io are three of the largest.*

6. *Ice*

7. *Troposphere; this is the lowest layer of the atmosphere, going up approximately 7 miles, contains 70% of the gases and the site of all the weather on Earth. As you move up through the troposphere, the stratosphere is where jet airplanes fly, then the mesophere. Temperature increases in the thermosphere because this layer absorbs much ultraviolet radiation. Gases are extremely thin in this layer, up to 190 miles up. Temperatures here are known to reach higher than 3,100 degrees, heated by the sun.*

GEOGRAPHY

1. How many years did it take to build the "Great Wall of China"?

2. What country has its own ruler, flag, currency and postage stamps, but it has no restaurants, pharmacies or hotels?

3. Monks in Germany created the pretzel; its shape was meant to represent what?

4. Where on earth is the major source of gold?

5. Athens, Greece was known as the birthplace of what form of government?

6. About 850 different languages are spoken in

_ _ _ _ _ _ _ _ _ _ _ _ _ _.

DID YOU KNOW:
Lake Nicaragua is the only freshwater lake in the world with sharks.

1. It took 1,700 years to build the "Great Wall", and this is about 4,000 miles long.

2. This is the Vatican City. It is the smallest country in the world. It is less than a quarter of a square mile or 110 acres.

3. A child's arms folded in prayer.

4. The Rand in South Africa. This was once a prehistoric lake.

5. Democracy.

6. Papua New Guinea

1. What is the longest mountain chain in the world? Hint: It is not in the Andes.

2. What is the only country in the world whose emergency telephone numbers consists entirely of 3 zeros?

3. Alaska is closer to this country (2 miles away at one point) than it is to the United States (500 miles away)?

4. What is the tallest waterfall in the world?

5. What state without a shore has a seagull as its state bird?

6. Where is most of the fresh water on Earth?

7. What is the country with the most official languages?

8. On Mount Rushmore, how long is George Washington's nose?

9. Where would you find the Bright Angel Trail?

1. The mid-ocean ridge, stretches 52,000 miles underneath the waters of the Atlantic, Pacific, Arctic and the Indian Oceans.

2. Australia. New Zealand's emergency number is 111.

3. Russia

DID YOU KNOW: Russia and Alaska are divided by the Bering Strait.

4. Angel Falls in South America is a little more than a 3,000 feet plunge. It is 15 times higher than Niagara Falls.

5. Utah. The Mormons adopted the California Sea Gull as its state bird.

6. Antarctica's ice caps

7. India, with 23

8. Twenty feet long. The mouth is 18 feet wide. The height of Mount Rushmore is 500 feet high and 400 feet wide. The President's faces are 60 feet tall.

9. This is the trail that leads to the bottom of the Grand Canyon.

1. Thousands of elephants were used in building the Taj Mahal; what were they hauling?

2. Ships traveling from the Atlantic to the Pacific or vice versa must pay about $50,000 to do what?

3. What river is 185 miles wide at its mouth?

a) Nile   b) Mississippi   c) Amazon

4. This country spans six time zones and has the longest coastline in the world at 151,400 miles?

5. What is the capital of West Virginia?

6. Where was the first oil well in the United States discovered?

7. What state capital was originally called Pig's Eye?

8. _ _ m _ _ r _ Street in London is equivalent to New York's W _ _ _ Street.

1. Two and a half ton slabs of marble

2. Pass through the Panama Canal. The Panama Canal is above sea level. To enter, ships must pass through a series of locks. Each year, more than 14,000 ships pass through the Panama Canal. A ship that is too big to pass through this canal is described as a "Post-Panamax."

3. c) Amazon. At almost 4,000 miles long, this outflow would fill about two million bathtubs every second. This river begins high up in the Peruvian Andes and runs mostly through Brazil and Peru.

4. Canada. Monaco has the shortest coastline at 3.5 miles.

5. Charleston

6. Titusville, Pennsylvania. Colonel Edwin Drake drilled the first oil well.

7. St. Paul, Minnesota. This was named after a man, Pierre "Pigs Eye" Parrant, who set up the first business there.

8. Lombard/Wall

DID YOU KNOW:
In the 1500s, April Fools Day began in France. They call this day "Poisson d'Avril which means "April Fish." This is what a victim of a hoax is called.

1. In 1903, the world's maximum speed limit for cars was set in _ _ n _ _ _, _ _ g _ a _ _ at 20 miles per hour.

2. In which country was the world's first paper money used?

a) China   b) Russia   c) United States

3. What river is the muddiest in the world?

4. What is the longest road on earth?

5. True or false; the natives of Monaco are called Monegasques?

6. What percentage of the Sahara Desert is covered by sand?

a) Twenty percent   b) Eighty percent
c) Ninety eight percent

7. What color are the swans in Australia?

8. In the 16th Century, donuts originated in what country?

1. *London, England*

2. *a) China; during the Song Dynasty in 1024.*

3. *Yellow River*

4. *The Pan-American Highway runs from Fairbanks, Alaska to Brazil.*

5. *True*

6. *a) Twenty percent*

7. *Black. These are native to Australia and Tasmania.*

8. *Holland. They were cooked in oil and were so greasy that the Dutch called them "Olykoeks."*

1. Name the bridge in the United States that was painted orange vermillion (international orange) since its inception in 1937?

2. What is the national currency that Ecuador, El Salvador and Panama use?

3. Where is the greatest deposit of copper in the world?

DID YOU KNOW:
Alaska has more earthquakes than the rest of the U.S. combined. They have as many as 4,000 a year.

4. 450 million years ago, the _ _ _ _ _ _
_ _ _ _ _ was where Antarctica is now and was covered in _ _ _.

5. From which language does Yiddish derive?

6. Which country did the French poodle originate?

7. Where is the windiest place on earth?

1. The Golden Gate Bridge has always been painted this color.

2. They use American dollars. Paraguay has no coinage, only paper money.

3. Chile. Andes Mountains

4. Sahara Desert ice

5. German.

6. Germany. A French poodle is a misnomer as this poodle originated in Germany as a water retriever. Then the French developed it to the modern breed it is today.

7. Commonwealth Bay, Antarctica. Speeds of 200 mph have been recorded.

DID YOU KNOW:
The largest Roman Catholic Cathedral in the United States is located on 5th Avenue, New York City; this is St. Patrick's Cathedral.
This is Gothic architecture.

ANIMALS

1. The only mammal that has a shell is the
_ _ _ _ _ _ _ _ _.

2. All Polar Bears are left-handed; true?

3. Where do fish get their oxygen?

4. Do turtles have teeth?

5. What color is the tongue of the giraffe?

6. How many legs does a lobster have?

   DID YOU KNOW:
   There's a fish called the Anableps fish. It
   has four eyes: two to see underwater, two
   to see above the surface.

7. Monkey and reindeer both like to
eat _ _ _ _ _ _ s.

1. Armadillo. Were you thinking the turtle? The turtle is not a mammal; it is a reptile.

2. True

3. Straight from the water

4. No teeth, but they do have a beak, and their jaws have horned ridges.

5. The tallest animal has a blue-black tongue, like the Chow dog. The giraffe sleeps for less than two hours a day. No need for a pillow because they sleep standing up!

6. 10; this includes its two front claws

7. Bananas

1. In their natural state, goldfish are what color?

2. Sharkskin is 100 times _ t _ _ _ g _ _ than cowhide.

3. Is it true female canaries cannot sing?

   DID YOU KNOW:
   Fire beetles (female) fly into forest fires to lay their eggs.

4. Where is a parson's nose on a chicken?

5. The fastest birds (flying) on earth are the _ _ _ _ g _ _ _ _ falcon and the _ p _ _ _ - _ _ i _ _ _ swift.

6. When do porcupines' quills get sharp?

7. What is the animal that has the most ribs?

1. *Olive green*

2. *Stronger*

3. *True*

4. *His rear end!*

5. *Peregrine falcon and the Spine-tailed Swift.*

6. *An hour or so after birth. When they are born, their quills are soft; then an hour later, they get hard.*

7. *The snake. His vertebrae is full of teeny tiny little bones which are his ribs.*

1. This mollusc's mouth is no larger than the size of a pin, but it has 25,000 teeth.

2. All living animals produce a small amount of what?

3. What is the only fish that can grab things with its (prehensile) tail?

4. This bird is 8 feet tall, weighs 300 pounds, and can cover 25 feet in a stride.

5. Where do the motmot birds build their nests?

6. Which animal moves by jet propulsion?

7. Which mammal migrates 12,000 miles annually from Mexico to the Bering Sea?

8. What is the largest fish?

9. Which mammal's tusk is almost half as long as its body? (lives in the Arctic)

1. Snail

2. Electricity

3. Seahorse

4. Ostrich. This is the fastest animal on two legs.

5. Underground. They come from Costa Rica.

6. Octopus. Their three main muscles allow this type of movement. Most live only one to two years.

7. Gray Whale

8. Whale shark. They are up to 46 feet, weighing up to 15 tons.

9. Narwhal

DID YOU KNOW:
A shark's skeleton is made of cartilage.

1. Why do spiders coat their legs with spittle?

2. Goats have no upper front a) _ _ _ _ _.
What they do have is one big tough gum and
_ _ w _ _ teeth.

3. Ants have _ _ _ _ noses. Each one smells a
different odor.

4. A bee has 5,000 _ _ _ _ _ _ _ _. It can smell
an apple tree two miles away.

5. A hen is capable of producing an egg every
25 _ _ _ _ _.

6. Poorwills, related to the whip-poor-will, are
one of few birds known to _ _ _ _ _ _ _ _ _.
(This is a small nightjar that is native to western
North America.)
These birds camouflage so well sitting amongst
the rocks in the desert regions.

7. What is the only animal that chews its food
with its legs?

1. *So they don't stick to their webs.*

2. *a) teeth b) lower*

3. *Five*

4. *Nostrils*

DID YOU KNOW: A bee has a lot in common with a starfish; both have five eyes. A starfish has five eyes, five arms and eats snails.

5. *Hours. A mother hen turns her egg approximately 50 times in a day. This is so the yolk does not stick to the shell.*

6. *Hibernate. Their body temperatures drop as much as 35 degrees, and they can be picked up without being aroused.*

7. *Horseshoe crab. They have no jaws to chew their food. They look the same as they did 300 million years ago.*

PLANTS

1. Where did the pineapple plant originate?

2. The vast majority of the world's greenery, that is 85 percent, lies in the Amazon rain forest; true or false?

3. Into which plant does the world's smallest owl, the elf owl, like to nest?

4. Where does cork come from?

5. What culinary flavoring is called "the stinking rose"?

6. A typical coffee tree produces how many pounds of coffee each year?

7. To which nut is poison ivy most closely related?

8. How did hammocks get their name?

   DID YOU KNOW:
   Those Redwood trees that grow approximately 300 feet tall, their seeds are so small that over 100,000 can fit into a one-pound bag.

1. South America. The first existence found in Hawaii was in the 19th Century.

2. Lies in the oceans. The plant life contained in the oceans of the world makes up 85% of all our greenery.

> DID YOU KNOW: Plants in the oceans produce over half of the world's oxygen.

3. Saguaro Cactus. Giant cactus of the American southwest

4. The bark of an evergreen oak tree.

5. Garlic. The Stinking Rose is a garlic restaurant out in California.

6. One pound takes about 4,000 hand-picked green coffee beans.

7. Cashew

> DID YOU KNOW: Poison oak is not an oak, and poison ivy is not an ivy.

8. They were first made from the fibers of the Hamack tree.

> DID YOU KNOW: The fastest growing plant on earth is bamboo. It can grow as much as three feet in a day.

FOOD/DRINK

1. What were bread crumbs once used for?

CAN YOU BELIEVE:

There's enough carbon in your body to make 900 pencil leads.

2. Do you know how Dr. Pepper got its name?

3. It takes approximately 600 grapes to make a
_ _ _ _ _ _ of wine.

4. What shape is Camembert cheese?

5. What fruit starts out as a stalk of a hundred or more flowers, and then these flowers fuse developing into this fruit?

6. How is Japan's rice wine, Sake, traditionally served?

7. Where did sweet corn originate?

1. To erase pencil marks

2. The chemist, Charles Alderton, named his drink after the father of a girl he was dating, Dr. Charles Kenneth Pepper.

3. Gallon. It takes 35 gallons of maple tree sap to make one gallon of maple syrup. It takes 25 tomatoes to make one bottle of ketchup.

4. Round

5. Pineapple

6. Sake is traditionally served warm in tiny porcelain cups.

7. Andes

DID YOU KNOW: When you eat a fig fruit, you are actually eating the flower.

FAMOUS PEOPLE

1. Name the actress that wanted to be a veterinarian, and her middle name is Fiona:

2. How many curls did Shirley Temple ALWAYS have in her hair?

DID YOU KNOW: Betsy Ross was born with a fully formed set of teeth.

3. Billionaire John D. Rockefeller frequently entertained guests by balancing _ _ _ _ _ _ _ _ on his nose.

4. Who wrote "I write the songs"? (it wasn't Barry Manilow)

5. Is it true that Robert Redford's father was a milkman?

6. Of the three stooges, who has the curliest hair?

7. What did Edgar Allen Poe and rock n' roller Jerry Lee Lewis have in common in their choice of wives?

1. *Julia Roberts*

2. *Exactly 56 curls*

3. *Crackers*

4. *Bruce Johnson*

5. *True. Later on, he was an accountant for Standard Oil.*

6. *Larry*

7. *Each married a 13-year-old cousin*

1. How old is Delta Dawn in the country and western song?

2. Actor _ _ _ _ _ _ _ _ _ _ was disqualified from the Navy's pilot training program during World War II because his blue eyes are color blind.

3. Name the type of hat Fred Astaire wore when he was "putting on the ritz"? (he wore this with his white tie and tails)

4. Is it true Ringo Starr was the youngest Beatle?

5. What was the price tag Minnie Pearl wore on her straw hat with artificial flowers?

6. How old was Stevie Wonder when he signed his first record contract?

7. Indiana Jones' first name was Harry; true or false?

1. *41*

2. *Paul Newman*

3. *Top hat. He made over a dozen movies wearing a "top hat." Abe Lincoln wore a variety of stovepipe hats of different heights.*

4. *No, George Harrison. Ringo was the oldest Beatle.*

5. *$1.98*

6. *11 years old. After an audition with Barry Gordy at Motown, he signed "Little Stevie Wonder" immediately.*

7. *No, he was born Henry Walton Jones, Jr. He first appeared in the 1981 movie "Raiders of the Lost Ark."*

HISTORY

1. The first coin-operated _ _ _ _ _ _ _
machines were in the 1930s.

2. What was the zipper first used on?

3. What did Thomas Watson receive on March
10, 1876?

4. What did Frank Whittle invent in 1930?

5. Who created the first post office, the daily
newspaper, the public library and the interstate
highway system?

6. Who was head of the FBI from 1924 to 1972?

7. On December 1963, how much did Frank
Sinatra pay in ransom for the release of his son's
kidnapping?

8. What was the first automobile to have
air-conditioning?

1. Pinball. Whiffle Board and Ballyhoo were the names of this type of gaming with the "clang of bells" and the "flip of flippers."

2. Shoes. In 1893, the zipper was invented by Whitcomb Judson. At first, this was called the "clasp locker". This invention came about because his friend had a stiff back and could not fasten his shoes. Whitcomb came up with a slide fastener that could be opened or closed with one hand. This was not very practical and many innovations were made before the zipper was a success.

3. The very first phone call ever. The famous first words were: Mr. Watson, come here, I want to see you...

4. Jet Engine

5. Benjamin Franklin. Also the lightning rod, etc.

6. Hoover

7. $240,000. Son was kidnapped on Dec 8th at Harrah's Lake Tahoe. On December 10th, 1963, two days later, he was returned.

8. Packard in 1939

1. Who was the original blonde bombshell?

2. How did grocers get their name?

3. The lollipop was named after _ _ _ _ _ _ _ _ _, one of the most famous _ _ _ _ _ _ _ _ _ _ _ of the early 1900s.

4. What year was paper money first introduced in the United States?

5. The _ _ _ _ _ _ _ _ _ _ in 1976 was the first U.S. military service academy to admit _ _ _ _ _.

6. The Berlin Wall stood for almost how many years?

7. Although Leonardo da Vinci had many designs for all types of inventions, what feat was he most proud of?

8. Name the statue that sculptor Bartholdi created.

1. Jean Harlow

2. They sold goods by the gross

3. Lolly Pop, race horses. This was one of the most famous racehorses of the 1900s. In the early 1900s, Mr. Smith was a candymaker from Connecticut, and he decided to put hard candy on a stick, and the Lollipop came about.

4. In 1690, Massachusettes Bay Colony issued the first paper money in the "13 colonies" which would later become the United States.

5. coast guard 1976 women

6. For almost 30 years, this wall stood from 1961 to 1989, splitting the city of Berlin into communist East Berlin and democratic West Berlin.

7. His ability to bend iron with his bare hands

8. Statue of Liberty. He used his mom's face and his girlfriend's body as a model for this statue.

1. Sailing from London to Shanghai, what was the cargo of the Cutty Sark when it made its maiden voyage in 1869?

DID YOU KNOW:
When traffic cones came out in 1914, they were first made out of concrete!

2. The first coast-to-coast paved road in the United States ran from New York to California. The year was 1913. Name this highway.

3. This type of stamp was first offered for sale in 1847.

4. In 1936, what were the price of a box of Girl Scout cookies when they debuted?

5. What is the national symbol of Ireland, and it is not the shamrock?

6. Martha Jane Bourke was the sharpshooter that preferred to wear pants. What was her more popular name?

1. Tea from China

2. The Lincoln Highway

3. Adhesive postage stamp (5 and 10 cent stamps)

4. They were 25 cents. Best-selling cookies are the thin mints.

5. It is the harp, and it has been since medieval times.

6. Calamity Jane. She performed work traditionally done by men.

DID YOU KNOW:
In the early 1800s, workers digging the Erie Canal were paid up to a dollar a day for a ten-hour-day. It is MOST surprising how straight this Canal is as they were also paid a quart of whiskey, and started drinking this at 6:00 a.m.

SPORTS

1. Name the New York Yankee that cooled down with cabbage leaves under his cap.

2. Baseball player Mickey Mantle batted
_ _ b _ _ _ x _ _ _ u_ _ _.

3. Name the three sword types that are used in fencing.

4. The driver is called a musher. Name this famous 1,299-mile, dog-sled race.

5. After the United States went undefeated in the America's Cup for over 100 years, who did we finally lose to in 1983?

6. A pole vaulter is allowed how many tries at each height?

7. Who was the only heavyweight boxing champion to retire undefeated?

8. Who did Muhammed Ali have to beat to become world champion in 1964?

1. Babe Ruth. This was his way of keeping cool. He changed these cabbage leaves every two innings.

DID YOU KNOW: In 1925, pinstripes were put on the uniforms of the New York Yankees to make the 260 pound "Bambino" (Babe Ruth) appear thinner!

2. Ambidextrously

3. The foil, epee and saber. This sport takes place on a narrow piste.

4. Iditarod. From Anchorage to Nome.

5. Australia. In 1851, the cup race started in Cowes, England. Ironically, they have never won this competition.

6. Three

7. Rocky Marciano won 49 fights and lost zero.

8. Sonny Liston

DID YOU KNOW:
Muhammad Ali was exiled from boxing for almost 4 years for not entering military service during the Vietnam War. In 1970, when he returned, he knocked out Jerry Quarry.

1. Who was nicknamed "The Georgia Peach," and what number did he wear?

2. In 1879, how many balls were required for a batter to "walk"?

3. What are the shrines called where Sumo wrestling is performed?

4. What sport are the "Queensbury Rules" written for?

DID YOU KNOW:
When the first regattas were held in the 17th Century, the vessels that were used were gondolas, and these races were held in Venice's Grand Canal.

5. What were the Yankees originally known as?

6. What are racetracks measured in?

1. Ty Cobb. This baseball legend didn't have a number on his jersey because he played before numbers were used.

2. Nine was required. Then in 1889, the number was reduced to four.

3. Shinto Shrines

4. Boxing. Written in 1867, these are the 12 rules of modern boxing. They were named after the Marquis of Queensbury.

5. The Highlanders. Their first stadium, Hilltop Park, was a wooden structure built on one of Manhattan's hills.

6. Furlongs. There are 8 furlongs in a mile.

DID YOU KNOW:
When Ben Hogan was a child, he overcame polio, and went on to become the greatest golfer of all time.

PRESIDENTS

1. President Obama has been known to have a serious s _ _ t b _ _ _ game. Although his daughter, Malia, is a great reader, she loves the H_ _ _ _ _ _ t t _ _ series. His specialty dish is his own _ _ i _ _.

2. Name the President who started the custom of the first baseball of the season being thrown.

3. In 1812, what was unusual about the surgery President Polk underwent for the removal of his gallstones?

4. Which President was always changing his clothes during the day, and he owned 80 pairs of pants?

5. During the "Roaring 20s," this President liked to take long naps during the day.

6. How did Abe Lincoln's mom die?

7. Name this President that was a short jolly Dutchman, and his favorite foods were oysters, doughnuts, raisins, figs and apples?

1. *Softball, Harry Potter, Chili*

2. *Taft*

3. *It was performed without the use of anesthetic.*

4. *Chester Arthur nicknamed "Elegant Arthur"*

5. *Calvin Coolidge. He was famous for taking long naps in the afternoons. He was a man of very few words, known as "Silent Cal."*

6. *When the family's dairy cow ate poisonous mushrooms, and she drank the milk.*

7. *Martin Van Buren*

DID YOU KNOW:
The only President to engage in a duel was President Andrew Jackson. On May 30, 1806, Andrew shot and killed Charles Dickinson. Charles made remarks that were unflattering toward Andrew's wife.

1. This most beloved Republican President, _ _ _ _ _ _   _ _ _ _ _ _ was knighted by Britain's Queen Elizabeth.

2. Which President, wife and daughter loved being together so much that they were given the moniker the "Three Musketeers"?

3. Why did President Woodrow Wilson win the Nobel Peace Prize in 1919?

4. Is it true Teddy Roosevelt set up the Declaration of Independence?

5. Nicknamed "Old Rough and Ready", this President died shortly after eating this? (Give his name and what he died of.)

6. 22nd and 24th, Grover Cleveland was the only "_ _ _ _ _ - _ _ _ _" President.

7. Give the name of this President that was known as the "Centennial President", "Kid Gloves", "Little Ben", and he had a goat named "Whiskers"?

1. Ronald Reagan. George Bush, Sr., and Ted Kennedy were also knighted by the Queen.

2. The Trumans - (Harry, Margaret and Bess). Harry sometimes joked that the threesome would have made a good vaudeville act.

3. Creating a lasting peace after World War I.

4. This is false. It was Thomas Jefferson. Also, he founded the Library of Congress.

5. Zachary Taylor. Eating cherries in a bowl. You might say he got the pits!

6. Split Term

7. Benjamin Harrison. He caused the "split term" for the above as he was #23.

DID YOU KNOW:
Dwight D. Eisenhower was the first President to see all 50 states, was the only one to serve in both World Wars and was the first President to have his pilot's license. (Hawaii, 50th state, entered union on August 21, 1959.)

1. How much did Lyndon Johnson pay for "Lady Bird's" wedding ring?

2. Who was the first President to live long enough to see his son become President? Year was 1825.

3. What did George Washington spend 7 percent of his $25,000 salary on?

4. President Ronald Reagan was born in Kentucky and then moved to Springfield, Illinois; true or false?

5. Which President was famous for saying "the buck stops here" and made the decision to drop the bomb on Japan?

6. During World War I, Edith Wilson decided to have these rather than wasting manpower to mow the lawn?

7. Which President set a record of shaking hands at a rate of 2,500 per hour?

DID YOU KNOW:
Ronald Reagan was nicknamed "Dutch" and his older brother Neil had the nickname "Moon", for his round face. They had these sobriquets when they were growing up.

1. This was purchased at Sears for $2.50.

2. John Adams. Wife didn't live long enough to see this.

3. Lots of alcohol

4. False. This was Abe Lincoln, born on a small farm near La Rue, Kentucky, spent his youth in Indiana and made Illinois his home.

5. Harry S. Truman. Year 1945.

6. Sheep were there to graze. She did this also for the production of wool.

7. President McKinley

MYTHOLOGY

1. Where did King Arthur keep court?

2. Aphrodite was the Greek goddess of _ _ _ _.

3. Phoenix was a fabulous winged horse; true?

4. True or false; King Arthur's sword was the Excalibur?

5. Which Greek God is Thursday named after?

6. The Golden Fleece was sought after by which Greek hero?

7. _ _ _ t _ _ _ was the Roman God of the sea.

8. Olaf was King of the Norse Gods; true or false?

9. What was the name of the island where Ulysses lived?

1. *Camelot*

2. *Love*

3. *False. It was Pegasus.*

4. *True*

5. *Thor*

6. *Jason*

7. *Neptune. Equivalent to the Greek God of the sea, Poseidon.*

8. *False. This was Odin*

9. *Ithaca*

DID YOU KNOW:
Pandora opened a box releasing all the ills; Vice, Plague, Spite, etc.

1. The Unicorn could be captured only by a what?

2. Everything Midas touched turned to silver; true or false?

3. The Amazons were very timid women; true?

4. What was Sir Galahad to Sir Lancelot?

5. Prometheus gave water to mortals; true?

6. Name the waterway you had to cross to get to Hades:

7. What King led the Greeks in the Trojan War?

8. What did Icarus fly too close to?

9. The Knights of the Round Table sought the _ _ _ _ _ _ _ _ _.

10. If you looked upon Helen of Troy, you turned to stone; true?

1. *Virgin*

2. *False. Turned to gold*

3. *False. They were warlike women*

4. *Sir Galahad was Sir Lancelot's son*

5. *False. He gave fire which he stole from Zeus.*

6. *The river Styx*

7. *Agamemnon. He was the brother of Menelaus. Agamemnon led an expedition against Troy to recover Helen. This started the Trojan War in which Paris was killed.*

8. *Sun. This melted the waxed wings that his father made for him.*

9. *Holy Grail*

10. *False. Medusa, one of the 3 gorgons. Helen of Troy was "The face that launched 1000 ships."*

DID YOU KNOW: Phoenix was the bird that was reborn from its own ashes.

WHERE IN THE WORLD...

ASIA

1. The isthmus of Kra separates the Gulf of Thailand from what sea?

2. From Singapore, if you wanted to travel to Brunei, what direction would you be traveling?

a) east b) west c) north d) south

3. How many stars are on the flag of East Timor?

4. How many islands are in Hong Kong?

a) less than 200 b) more than 200

5. What is the country that lies below China and borders India, Thailand and Laos?

6. What is the capital of Myanmar?

7. Name this country that has the most Muslims, it starts with an "I", and it is not India?

1. *Andaman Sea*

2. *a) East. Singapore is at the southern tip of Asia. This small country is one of the world's busiest harbors.*

3. *One 5-pointed white star in the center of a black triangle.*

4. *b) more than 200. There are 235. Most are uninhabited; while those which are inhabited have a way of life that has remained the same for decades.*

5. *Myanmar.*

6. *Burma. This country has more child soldiers than any other nation.*

7. *Indonesia, then Pakistan, India, Bangladesh and Turkey*

People who practice Islam are called Muslims.

EUROPE

1. Oktoberfest is a Polish holiday; true?

2. In which city would you find Capitoline Hill?

a) Paris b) Rome c) London

3. The Matterhorn lies in _ _ _ _ z _ _ _ _ _ _ _
and _ _ a _ _.

4. What sea separates Greece from Turkey?

a) Black Sea b) Aegean Sea c) Mediterranean

5. From Turkey to the Carpathian Mountains,
which way would you travel?

a) North   b) South   c) East

6. Does Aberdeen lie on the east or west coast
of Scotland?

7. What sea separates Sudan from Saudi Arabia?

1. False. This is Germany. Oktoberfest is the largest beer festival in the world, held in Munich.

2. b) Rome. This is the highest of the seven hills in Rome.

3. Switzerland/Italy

4. b) Aegean Sea

5. a) North

6. East coast on North Sea

7. Red Sea

DID YOU KNOW:
The reason the Mediterranean Sea has no tides is because it is surrounded by land.

AFRICA

1. The Kanembu tribe live on the shores of Lake Chad in Africa. The staple food they harvest from this lake is algae, a common variety known as spirulina. They dry this on the sand, mix it up into a spicy cake; this is eaten with tomatoes and chili peppers. This lake is between the countries of N _ _ _ _ and S _ _ _ _.

> DID YOU KNOW:
> Although Africa is the warmest continent, it has snow on a few of its alps.

2. The _ _ _ _ _ _ Desert stretches further than the distance from _ _ _ _ _ o _ _ _ a to _ _ _ _ _ r _ . This Desert in Africa is almost the same size as the _ _ _ _ e _ _ _ a _ _ _.

3. Which African country is closest to Spain?

4. What is the color star on Djibouti's flag?

5. Name the grassland in Kenya and Tanzania where about two million animals migrate each year.

1. *Niger and Sudan*

2. *Sahara California New York United States*

3. *Morocco*

4. *Red stands for unity*

5. *Serengeti*

STATES

1. Name the cave in southern Indiana that has the largest mountain - underground?

2. In Death Valley, California, what is the average yearly rainfall?

3. Name the mountain range that runs through Oregon and Washington. HINT: This has the same name as a waterfall.

4. What is the state with the most lakes, and it is not Minnesota?

5. In 1867, when U.S. Secretary of State William Seward bought Alaska for two cents an acre, people believed the state was worthless, so they called it "S _ _ _ _ _ 's _ _ _ _ _".

> DID YOU KNOW:
> Alaskan residents don't have to pay any income tax because the state makes lots of money from its oil fields.

6. My state capital is considered the "live music capital of the world". More wool comes from my state than any other state. The majority of my rivers empty into the Gulf of Mexico. Which state am I?

1. This is the Wyandotte Cave. This mountain is at 135 feet high.

2. Less than 2 inches. 1.5 inches is all the rainfall this valley gets. This is the lowest point in the U.S., Death Valley, America's highest known temperature at 144 degrees.

3. Cascade Mountain Range. This is known as the "Switzerland of North America", the location of Mount Rainier, the highest peak in the state of Washington, at 14,410 feet; this is a dormant volcano. Mount Rainier and Mount St. Helens are part of the Cascade Mountain Range.
Many people that live in this state live in cities and towns that directly border Puget Sound.

4. Alaska. More than 3 million lakes compared with Minnesota's "The Land of 10,000 lakes."

5. Seward's Folly turned out to be Sewards' foresight. No folly here! Both gold and oil were discovered in this "Land of the Midnight Sun". Alaska has over 3,000 rivers!

6. Austin/Texas

LARGEST COUNTRIES

1. The largest country in the world is _ _ _ _ _ _, borders 13 countries.

2. _ _ _ _ _ _ is the second largest country in the world, has one neighbor, the United States.

3. _ _ _ _ _ is the worlds' third largest country, by land size. It borders 14 countries.

4. _ _ _ _ _ _ _ _ _ _ _ is the fourth largest country, and it has two neighbors, _ _ _ _ _ _ and _ _ _ _ _ _.

1. *Russia*

2. *Canada*

3. *China*

4. *United States Canada Mexico*

FUN FACTS

The original name of the Xerox Corporation was the Haloid Company.

An Italian deck of cards has no queens.

A bison can jump as high as six feet off the ground, and it weighs more than one ton.

Dr. Elbert Dysart Botts invented the raised-bump reflectors on the United States' roads. These are called Botts' Dots.

Shakespeare's family were all illiterate.

Beavers sometimes get crushed by the trees they gnaw down.

The original name for Goldilocks was Silver Hair, then Silverlocks, then Goldilocks.

In Japan, you can rent a dog as a companion for $20.00 an hour.

Superglue does not stick to the bottle because it needs oxygen to set and there's no oxygen in the bottle.

The collective name for a group of goats is called a "trip".

Birds' bones weigh less than their feathers.

The Earth's shape is not round; it is an oblate spheroid. It has an oblong appearance because there's a bulge from pole to pole.

Santa travels on a goat in the country of Finland. The goat's name is Ukko!

Hippopotami are born underwater.

The low man on the totem pole is the most important man in the tribe, contrary to the popular saying.

Frank Sinatra's father, Marty Sinatra, once boxed under the name Marty O'Brien. This was in the 1920s.

Sliced bread was introduced in 1930.

The sound a goose makes is a honk.

DO YOU REMEMBER

THE SEVENTIES:

Star Wars' action figures

Gee Your Hair Smells Terrific

Leisure Suits

Dorothy Hamil haircuts

The Hustle (dance)

Mood Rings

Mr. Whipple ("Please don't squeeze the Charmin")

THE EIGHTIES:

Atari

Aqua Net Hairspray

Care Bears

Shasta soda

Scrunch socks

Bandana ties around one's leg

Smurfs

Penny Loafers

THINGS THAT MAKE YOU GO HMMM!

Why do we wait until a pig is dead to "cure" it?

Why buy a product that takes 2000 flushes to get rid of?

What is another word for synonym?

If a stealth bomber crashes in a forest, does it make a sound?

If a turtle loses its shell, does that mean he's naked or homeless?

How come sheep don't shrink when it rains?

If a parsley farmer is sued, can they garnish his wages?

Where do forest rangers go to get away from it all?

If the cop arrests a mime, do they say to him, he has the right to remain silent?

Thank you, see you later, alligator!!!

Made in the USA
San Bernardino, CA
18 December 2012